HAPPY TIME

(On S'Amuse Au Piano)

by ALEXANDRE TANSMAN

Contents

ISBN: 978-0-7935-1299-7

HAL•LEONARD®
CORPORATION
7777 W. BLUEMOUND RD. P.O. BOX 13819 MILWAUKEE, WI 53213

Visit Hal Leonard Online at
www.halleonard.com

Little Prelude

Petit Prélude

Alexandre Tansman

Moderato

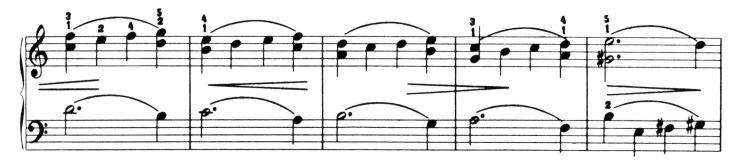

Dancing Air
Air à Danser

Alexandre Tansman

Vivo

Slow Waltz
Valse-Boston

Alexandre Tansman

Allegretto grazioso

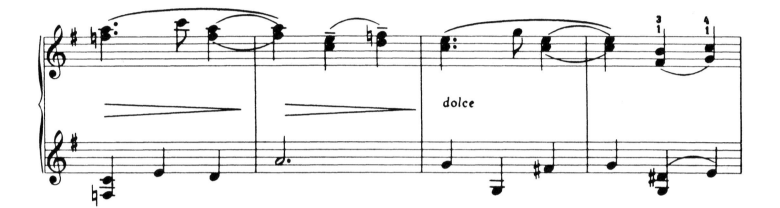

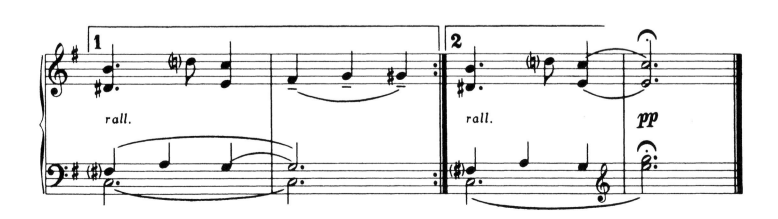

Caravan
Caravane

Alexandre Tansman

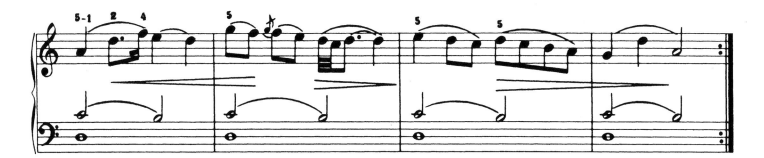

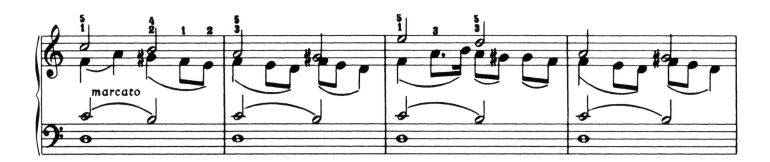

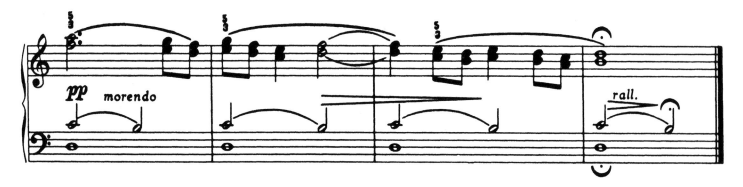

Versailles
Versailles

Alexandre Tansman

Tempo di menuetto

Lament
Plainte

Alexandre Tansman

Lento cantabile

Perpetual Motion
Moto Perpetuo

Alexandre Tansman

Vivo

Four Voices
À Quatre Voix

Alexandre Tansman

Lento cantabile

Pursuit
Poursuite

Alexandre Tansman

Allegro con moto

Chorale and Variation
Choral Varié

Alexandre Tansman

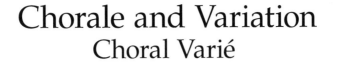

Study
Étude

Alexandre Tansman

Choral
Choral

Alexandre Tansman

Swedish Dance
Danse Suédoise

Alexandre Tansman